POEMS *to* LIVE BY

In Troubling Times

"POEMS

to

LIVE BY

In Troubling Times //

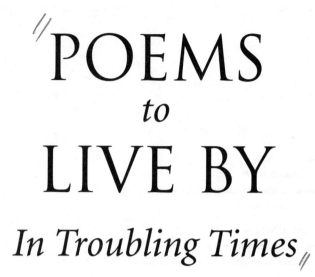

EDITED BY *Joan Murray*

BEACON PRESS
BOSTON

Beacon Press
25 Beacon Street
Boston, Massachusetts 02108-2892
www.beacon.org

Beacon Press books
are published under the auspices of
the Unitarian Universalist Association of Congregations.

09 08 07 06   8 7 6 5 4 3 2 1

This book is printed on acid-free paper that meets the uncoated
paper ANSI/NISO specifications for permanence as revised in 1992.

Design and composition by Wilsted & Taylor Publishing Services

Library of Congress Control Number 2006900305

Acknowledgment of permission to reprint
copyrighted material begins on page 143.

To the 3000 people killed in the 2001 terror attacks,
and the 250 U.S. soldiers killed in Afghanistan.

And to the more than 2100 U.S. soldiers
and more than 30,000 Iraqi civilians
killed since the United States invaded Iraq.

May history judge us gently
for how we guarded and honored them.

CONTENTS

VI. A Prayer That Will Be Answered
Meditation and Prayer

VII. I Gave Away That Kid
War and Violence

VIII. Ourselves Again
Peace and Justice

INTRODUCTION

It's hard to believe that nearly five years have passed since September 11—a date that needs no year attached to it. Even if we sometimes refer to the events of that day as "the terror attacks," our minds keep insisting on the phrase "September 11." Two everyday words. But say them together with your eyes shut, and you'll summon up nightmare visions and merciless emotions that will make your heart race to escape.

Some words can be *that* powerful.

I think we've been trying very hard to escape September 11. Maybe because it entered our lives in such a sudden, devastating, and demanding way. It catapulted us from our sense of comfort and entitlement. For a short time we met its challenge in our outpourings of sympathy and generosity, in our soul-searchings and the resolutions that followed, and in our new awareness of mortality and the consequences it had for our lives. But such intense engagement with each other, with ourselves, and with life and death can be pretty exhausting.

Maybe that's why we soon seemed overwhelmed. After we held our ceremonies and broke ground for our memorials, we handed the course of our future to our institutions and headed home to the silence to catch our breath.

Yet many powerful words have been spoken since September 11. Some have been quiet goodbyes in small-town graveyards, where flag-draped coffins come home without a nation's acknowledgment. Others have been pleas for rescue from deluged rooftops in New Orleans. Others have been carping accusations from careerist politicians too afraid to take the risks to lead us. And others have been lies—lies that have put our soldiers' lives, and perhaps our democracy, in danger.

These days I keep thinking of Talleyrand's line: "Speech was given to man to disguise his thoughts." It's been difficult to know when we're being deceived because teams of highly paid speech writers are engaged to manipulate our approval. No wonder so many of us have grown anxious. We've grown uncertain about what to believe—and uncertain what to do about it.

But here's a bit of good news: We're not alone. Voices are calling out to us from times and places at least as troubled as our own. They're the voices of poets of our own era, and I've gathered the most compelling of them in this book.

Some readers may know the anthology that preceded this one: *Poems to Live By in Uncertain Times.* That book grew out of a poem I read on National Public Radio's *Morning Edition* eight days after the attacks. It was a spontaneous anthem to those who'd died and to those who came forward to help. It was called "Survivors Found," and the point of it was that we had gone through the fires of that day and had emerged in a different place: we were in pain, yet unbroken, tempered by the flames and—with our pettiness and differences stripped away—we were such a promising nation.

Nearly ten thousand people asked for copies of that poem. For people like them—people who *needed* poetry then—I began to assemble my anthology. Miraculously, I had it in hand two months later: on

November 11, I read from it, surrounded by firemen—some of whom had escaped the World Trade Center's collapse, and others who had dug through its rubble to recover what remained. Later I read from *Poems to Live By in Uncertain Times* at a retreat for peace activists, at a military base, at a stamp unveiling in a stadium, and at New York state's anniversary observance. Yet I remember that first reading because all those many people, such good, brave people, came up to thank me for *poems.*

What helped me have that book for them that day (besides the miracles Beacon Press worked) was a binder I'd kept for many years called "Poems to Live By." I'd formed a habit of putting "necessary" poems into that binder so I could turn to them in times of difficulty or celebration. (Often, I'd choose a poem for some friend who could use it.) That binder became the basis for my first anthology—as well as for this one.

The times we face now are much more troubling than the days following September 11—when we were sorrowful and anxious but also generous and renewed. Now fear dominates us—crippling us, silencing us, directing our vote, urging us to suspect each other, leading us into an endless war with a murky, ubiquitous enemy. Now we've begun to realize the awful costs—human, economic, and moral—of our hasty, misdirected, unnecessary invasion. Now our leaders follow us—until they're ready to lead us.

To face these troubling times, I've been turning to a new group of necessary poems—some I gathered long ago, some I've discovered in the past five years, and some that friends and strangers have sent to me. These poems challenge me and comfort me; they alarm me and encourage me; they rouse my anger and stir my hope. That's why I need them.

I need the words of Seamus Heaney to delineate how it feels to be a suspect in your own land. I need the words of Anne Sexton to persuade me to take genuine risks, and the words of Stephen Dunn to remind me what we've lost. I need the words of Nazim Hikmet to show me the value of living—or even dying— for others.

I need the words of Ernesto Cardenal to give me the courage to hold our leaders accountable. I need Alicia Ostriker to help me pray when I don't believe. I need Ursula Le Guin to spell out why our new war is unlike all the ones our parents fought. I need Derek

Walcott to help me imagine peace so intensely that it almost happens. And I need Yehuda Amichai to help me rise out of my frightened, barricaded self and embrace justice.

I need these words—as I imagine you do—to help me cut through the daily muddle of rhetoric being handed down by people who seem at least as lost as we are—or, worse, by those who cling to the wreckage of their ambitions and will pull us down with them.

But in the midst of all that desperate noise, the words of poets—the intimate, honest, urgent words of poets who've come through their own troubling times—can help us see clearly. They can rouse us from our torpor and persuade us to act. They can help us restore ourselves—and reclaim our nation.

Some words can be *that* powerful.

Joan Murray

I

IN TRYING TIMES

Anxiety and Terror

Nocturne

❧ LI-YOUNG LEE

That scraping of iron on iron when the wind
rises, what is it? Something the wind won't
quit with, but drags back and forth.
Sometimes faint, far, then suddenly, close, just
beyond the screened door, as if someone there
squats in the dark honing his wares against
my threshold. Half steel wire, half metal wing,
nothing and anything might make this noise
of saws and rasps, a creaking and groaning
of bone-growth, or body-death, marriages of rust,
or ore abraded. Tonight, something bows
that should not bend. Something stiffens that should
slide. Something, loose and not right,
rakes or forges itself all night.

A Suitcase Strapped with a Rope

CHARLES SIMIC

*T*hey made themselves so small
They could all fit in a suitcase.
The suitcase they kept under the bed,
And the bed near the open window.

They just huddled there in the dark
While the mother called out the names
To make sure no one was missing.
Her voice made them so warm, made them
    so sleepy.

He wanted to go out and play.
He even said so once or twice.
They told him to be quiet.
Just now the suitcase was moving.

Soon the border guards were going
To open it up,
Unless of course it was a thief
And he had a long way to go.

From the Frontier of Writing

∽ SEAMUS HEANEY

*T*he tightness and the nilness round that space
when the car stops in the road, the troops inspect
its make and number and, as one bends his face

towards your window, you catch sight of more
on a hill beyond, eyeing with intent
down cradled guns that hold you under cover

and everything is pure interrogation
until a rifle motions and you move
with guarded unconcerned acceleration—

a little emptier, a little spent
as always by that quiver in the self,
subjugated, yes, and obedient.

So you drive on to the frontier of writing
where it happens again. The guns on tripods;
the sergeant with his on-off mike repeating

data about you, waiting for the squawk
of clearance; the marksman training down
out of the sun upon you like a hawk.

And suddenly you're through, arraigned yet freed,
as if you'd passed from behind a waterfall
on the black current of a tarmac road

past armour-plated vehicles, out between
the posted soldiers flowing and receding
like tree shadows into the polished windscreen.

In Trying Times

~ Heberto Padilla

*Translated from the Spanish
by Alastair Reid and Andrew Hurley*

*T*hey asked that man for his time
so that he could link it to History.
They asked him for his hands,
because for trying times
nothing is better than a good pair of hands.
They asked him for his eyes
that once had tears
so that he should see the bright side
(the bright side of life, especially)
because to see horror one startled eye is enough.
They asked him for his lips,
parched and split, to affirm,
to belch up, with each affirmation, a dream
(the great dream)
they asked him for his legs
hard and knotted
(his wandering legs)

because in trying times
is there anything better than a pair of legs
for building or digging ditches?
They asked him for the grove that fed him as a child,
with its obedient tree.
They asked him for his breast, heart, his shoulders.
They told him
that that was absolutely necessary.
They explained to him later
that all this gift would be useless
unless he turned his tongue over to them,
because in trying times
nothing is so useful in checking hatred or lies.
And finally they begged him,
please, to go take a walk.
Because in trying times
that is, without a doubt, the decisive test.

Out in the Open (Part II)

    Tomas Tranströmer

Translated from the Swedish by Robert Bly

A letter from America drove me out again, started
    me walking
through the luminous June night in the empty
    suburban streets
among newborn districts without memories, cool
    as blueprints.

Letter in my pocket. You wild, raging, walking, you
    are a kind of prayer for others.
Over there evil and good actually have faces.
With us for the most part it's a fight between roots,
    numbers, shades of light.

The people who do death's errands don't shy from
    daylight.
They rule from glass offices. They mill about in the
    bright sun.
They lean forward over a table, and throw a look
    to the side.

Far off I found myself standing in front of one of the new
  buildings.
Many windows flowed together there into a single
  window.
The luminous night sky was caught in it, and the walking
  trees.
It was a mirror-like lake with no waves, turned on edge
  in the summer night.

Violence seemed unreal.
For a few moments.

The Terrorist, He Watches

WISŁAWA SZYMBORSKA

Translated from the Polish
by Robert A. Maguire
and Magnus Jan Krynski

The bomb will go off in the bar at one twenty p.m.
Now it's only one sixteen p.m.
Some will still have time to get in,
some to get out.

The terrorist has already crossed to the other side of
    the street.
The distance protects him from any danger,
and what a sight for sore eyes:

A woman in a yellow jacket, she goes in.
A man in dark glasses, he comes out.
Guys in jeans, they are talking.
One seventeen and four seconds.
That shorter guy's really got it made, and gets on a
    scooter,
and that taller one, he goes in.

One seventeen and forty seconds.
That girl there, she's got a green ribbon in her hair.
Too bad that bus just cut her off.
One eighteen p.m.
The girl's not there any more.
Was she dumb enough to go in, or wasn't she?
That we'll see when they carry them out.

One nineteen p.m.
No one seems to be going in.
Instead a fat baldy's coming out.
Like he's looking for something in his pockets and
at one nineteen and fifty seconds
he goes back for those lousy gloves of his.

It's one twenty p.m.
The time, how it drags.
Should be any moment now.
Not yet.
Yes, this is it.
The bomb, it goes off.

Dedications to Bashert

❧ IRENA KLEPFISZ

These words are dedicated to those who died

*T*hese words are dedicated to those who died
because they had no love and felt alone in the world
because they were afraid to be alone and tried to stick
    it out
because they could not ask
because they were shunned
because they were sick and their bodies could not
    resist the disease
because they played it safe
because they had no connections
because they had no faith
because they felt they did not belong and wanted
    to die

These words are dedicated to those who died
because they were loners and liked it
because they acquired friends and drew others to
    them
because they took risks
because they were stubborn and refused to give up
because they asked for too much

These words are dedicated to those who died
because a card was lost and a number was skipped
because a bed was denied
because a place was filled and no other place was left

These words are dedicated to those who died
because someone did not follow through
because someone was overworked and forgot
because someone left everything to God

because someone was late
because someone did not arrive at all
because someone told them to wait and they just
    couldn't any longer
These words are dedicated to those who died
because death is a punishment

because death is a reward
because death is the final rest
because death is eternal rage

These words are dedicated to those who died

Bashert

These words are dedicated to those who survived

These words are dedicated to those who survived
because their second grade teacher gave them books
because they did not draw attention to themselves
     and got lost
in the shuffle
because they knew someone who knew someone
     else who could
help them and bumped them into a corner on a
     Thursday
afternoon
because they played it safe
because they were lucky

These words are dedicated to those who survived
because they knew how to cut corners
because they drew attention to themselves and always got
picked
because they took risks
because they had no principles and were hard

These words are dedicated to those who survived
because they refused to give up and defied statistics
because they had faith and trusted in God
because they expected the worst and were always prepared
because they were angry
because they could ask
because they mooched off others and saved their strength
because they endured humiliation
because they turned the other cheek
because they looked the other way

These words are dedicated to those who survived
because life is a wilderness and they were savage
because life is an awakening and they were alert
because life is a flowering and they blossomed

because life is a struggle and they struggled
because life is a gift and they were free to accept it

These words are dedicated to those who survived

Bashert

The Measures Taken

ERICH FRIED

*Translated from the German
by Michael Hamburger*

The lazy are slaughtered
the world grows industrious

The ugly are slaughtered
the world grows beautiful

The foolish are slaughtered
the world grows wise

The sick are slaughtered
the world grows healthy

The sad are slaughtered
the world grows merry

The old are slaughtered
the world grows young

The enemies are slaughtered
the world grows friendly

The wicked are slaughtered
the world grows good.

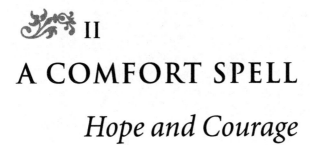 II

A COMFORT SPELL

Hope and Courage

Heart Labor

MAGGIE ANDERSON

When I work too hard and then lie down,
even my sleep is sad and all worn out.
You want me to name the specific sorrows?
They do not matter. You have your own.
Most of the people in the world
go out to work, day after day,
with their voices chained in their throats.
I am swimming a narrow, swift river.
Upstream, the clouds have already darkened
and deep blue holes I cannot see
churn up under the smooth flat rocks.
The Greeks have a word, *paropono*,
for the complaint without answer,
for how the heart labors, while
all the time our faces appear calm
enough to float through in the moonlight.

A Comfort Spell

MAXINE SILVERMAN

I.

My father's teeth gap slightly.
Easy to spit seeds,
a natural grace.

II.

"Pa," I write, "I'm low."
"Better soon," he swears. "Soon. Soon.
You're talkin to one who knows."

Lord, it's nearly time. October.
He'll pick some leaves off our sugar maples,
pressed, send them to New York.
Flat dry leaves,
and rusty rich.
Pa stays in Missouri,
bets the underdog each tv game,
and the home team, there or away.

"Lord," he whistles through his teeth,
"that boy's a runnin fool. Mercy me."

He names himself:
Patrick O'Silverman,
one of the fightinest!

Melancholy crowds him spring and fall,
regular
seasonal despair,
his brain shocked, his smile fraught with prayer.
I offer what remains of my childhood.
I offer up this comfort spell.

Whoever you are, run in nearly morning
to the center of the park.
There, rooted in the season,
maples send out flame.
Gather you to the river the furious leaf.
Mercy
Mercy Buck Up
Mercy Me
Mercy
Mercy Buck Up
Mercy Me

"Pa," I call, "what's new?"
"Nothin much. We're gettin on."

"Pa," I sing, "your leaves came today."
"Oh Maggie," he cries, "just want
to share the fall."

Making a Fist

Naomi Shihab Nye

We forget that we are all dead
men conversing with dead men.
   —Jorge Luis Borges

For the first time, on the road north of Tampico,
I felt the life sliding out of me,
a drum in the desert, harder and harder to hear.
I was seven, I lay in the car
watching palm trees swirl a sickening pattern past
   the glass.
My stomach was a melon split wide inside my skin.

"How do you know if you are going to die?"
I begged my mother.
We had been traveling for days.
With strange confidence she answered,
"When you can no longer make a fist."

Years later I smile to think of that journey,
the borders we must cross separately,
stamped with our unanswerable woes.
I who did not die, who am still living,
still lying in the backseat behind all my questions,
clenching and opening one small hand.

Healing

∾   D. H. LAWRENCE

I am not a mechanism, an assembly of various
     sections.
And it is not because the mechanism is working
     wrongly, that I am ill.
I am ill because of wounds to the soul, to the deep
     emotional self
and the wounds to the soul take a long, long time,
     only time can help
and patience, and a certain difficult repentance
long, difficult repentance, realisation of life's
     mistake, and the freeing oneself
from the endless repetition of the mistake
which mankind at large has chosen to sanctify.

Spell Against Sorrow

❧ KATHLEEN RAINE

Who will take away
Carry away sorrow,
Bear away grief?

Stream wash away
Float away sorrow,
Flow away, bear away
Wear away sorrow,
Carry away grief.

Mists hide away
Shroud my sorrow,
Cover the mountains,
Overcloud remembrance,
Hide away grief.

Earth take away
Make away sorrow,
Bury the lark's bones
Under the turf.
Bury my grief.

Black crow tear away
Rend away sorrow,
Talon and beak
Pluck out the heart
And the nerves of pain,
Tear away grief.

Sun take away
Melt away sorrow,
Dew lies grey,
Rain hangs on the grass,
Sun dry tears.

Sleep take away
Make away sorrow,
Take away the time,
Fade away place,
Carry me away
From the world of my sorrow.

Song sigh away
Breathe away sorrow,
Words tell away,
Spell away sorrow,
Charm away grief.

The Sun

~ MARY OLIVER

*H*ave you ever seen
anything
in your life
more wonderful

than the way the sun,
every evening,
relaxed and easy,
floats toward the horizon

and into the clouds or the hills,
or the rumpled sea,
and is gone—
and how it slides again

out of the blackness,
every morning,
on the other side of the world,
like a red flower

streaming upward on its heavenly oils,
say, on a morning in early summer,
at its perfect imperial distance—
and have you ever felt for anything

such wild love—
do you think there is anywhere, in any language,
a word billowing enough
for the pleasure

that fills you,
as the sun
reaches out,
as it warms you

as you stand there,
empty-handed—
or have you too
turned from this world—

or have you too
gone crazy
for power,
for things?

Happiness

❧ JANE KENYON

There's just no accounting for happiness,
or the way it turns up like a prodigal
who comes back to the dust at your feet
having squandered a fortune far away.

And how can you not forgive?
You make a feast in honor of what
was lost, and take from its place the finest
garment, which you saved for an occasion
you could not imagine, and you weep night and day
to know that you were not abandoned,
that happiness saved its most extreme form
for you alone.

No, happiness is the uncle you never
knew about, who flies a single-engine plane
onto the grassy landing strip, hitchhikes
into town, and inquires at every door

until he finds you asleep midafternoon
as you so often are during the unmerciful
hours of your despair.

It comes to the monk in his cell.
It comes to the woman sweeping the street
with a birch broom, to the child
whose mother has passed out from drink.
It comes to the lover, to the dog chewing
a sock, to the pusher, to the basket maker,
and to the clerk stacking cans of carrots
in the night.
    It even comes to the boulder
in the perpetual shade of pine barrens,
to rain falling on the open sea,
to the wineglass, weary of holding wine.

Riding the Elevator into the Sky

୬   ANNE SEXTON

*A*s the fireman said:
Don't book a room over the fifth floor
in any hotel in New York.
They have ladders that will reach further
but no one will climb them.
As the New York *Times* said:
The elevator always seeks out
the floor of the fire
and automatically opens
and won't shut.
These are the warnings
that you must forget
if you're climbing out of yourself.
If you're going to smash into the sky.

Many times I've gone past
the fifth floor,
cranking upward,

but only once
have I gone all the way up.
Sixtieth floor:
small plants and swans bending
into their grave.
Floor two hundred:
mountains with the patience of a cat,
silence wearing its sneakers.
Floor five hundred:
messages and letters centuries old,
birds to drink,
a kitchen of clouds.
Floor six thousand:
the stars,
skeletons on fire,
their arms singing.
And a key,
a very large key,
that opens something—
some useful door—
somewhere—
up there.

III

THOSE DESTROYED
by SUCCESS

*Complacency
and Complicity*

Whenever That Happened

BRENDAN KENNELLY

*H*ell is the familiar all stripped of wonder.
Was there a moment
When wonder at the world died in my eyes?
Had I a friend I could recognize?
When did I take friendship for granted?
When did I get used to the thought of murder?
When did my flesh cease to astonish me?
When did my mind become gray-familiar?
Whenever that happened is when I knew
I could do anything.
When wonder died in me power was born.
I can change the world because I no longer dream of
    blue,
I can betray a god because I never heard a girl sing
Of steps in the street or sunlight blessing a field of
    corn.

Crash

DAVID COPE

*t*he cars lie, one on its side,
a rear wheel still spinning,
& the other upside down.
the bodies are scattered across the cornfield,
bent & broken on the frozen ground.
two ambulances pull up.
the attendants arrange & cover the dead.
cars pull over to the side of the road,
everyone shuffles,
eager to help, hands in pockets.

Intrusion

◌◟   DENISE LEVERTOV

After I had cut off my hands
and grown new ones

something my former hands had longed for
came and asked to be rocked.

After my plucked out eyes
had withered, and new ones grown

something my former eyes had wept for
came asking to be pitied.

Scruples

∿ STEPHEN DUNN

* * *

Since the early eighties more students in my Literature & Ethics class, a freshman seminar, say they would press a button that would kill a nondescript peasant in another land, for which they would receive one million dollars and the guarantee of never being caught. They respond anonymously and must give a reason. Four out of twenty-five would in 1982. Eleven out of twenty-five in 1995. Reasons: Because it would set me up for life. Or, It's just a one-time thing. And once, Because it's a doggie-dog world. Afterward, I point out that the question is designed only to see if they are murderers. By semester's end, I'm pretty sure I know who they are, these murderers, and it all switches to me—that age-old imperative, to discover what's right and to do it. I've given a murderer an A because of incontrovertible intelligence. Yet I've graded down at least a few because their logic, however sound, was without heart and I didn't like their faces. And I can't say how many times I've given up on some of the decent ones—their correct, inherited, annoying positions unchanged by drama or dialectic. In the early seventies, no one I knew would press the button. I love that it wasn't high-mindedness back then, merely the obvious, and that so many wished to do good. Experience took years to show us what we could not sustain.

FROM *Twelve Chairs*

ɔ RITA DOVE

Fourth Juror

Cancel the afternoon
evenings mornings all
the days to come
until the fires
fall to ash
the fog clears
and we can see
where we
really
stand.

Fifth Juror

How long will
this take?
I am not my
brother,

thank you;
my hands are
full already
taking care
of
myself.

Twelfth Juror

why is the rose
how is the sun
where is first
when is last
who will
love us
what
will
save
us

The Alternate

—And who are you?
—*Nobody.*
—What do you do?
—*I am alive.*
—But who'll vouch
for you?
—*Listen closely,*
you'll hear
the
wind.

Those Destroyed by Success

〜 WILLIAM DICKEY

*T*he very large pasteboard replica of the general,
his medals pasted from his chest
down over his washboard belly,
is propped up at the podium and squeaks.
Skillful technicians amplify and dilute
what he appears to be saying, until the audience,
which is comatose anyway from the brandy
and the smuggled cigars, grunts
approvingly into its paunches.
It will be all right.

Even the general, even the president,
who is weeping in the Oval Office
at the thought of having to give up
the least hangnail of power, even
the great poet whose voice has become
so identifiable that we genuflect
hearing it, shutting off our minds
to the recognition that it is only a voice now,

even these, before their success, were men.
Inside them, as they are towed, great
helium balloons in the Macy's Christmas parade,
there may still be men rattling,
but how are we to know?

I watch you ricochet
from banquet to banquet, from
radio to talk show, and I think
"That is my friend. She is in
real danger." And you watch me
in a suit with a vest, and wearing a
Countess Mara tie, accepting
with judicious well-phrased thanks.

Both of us need to remember that
we are no good, no good, really.
Neither of us can speak fluent Greek.
Both of us can cook, but last night
I ruined a perfectly possible chicken soup,
and I still remember when your stove caught fire
and you had to redecorate the kitchen.

To be destroyed by success, I think
you do need to begin to believe

you can do anything and everything
and as the belief grows
little bits of the brain fall off
and turn into recalcitrant diamonds.
And eventually you are only a scatter of diamond
and a hollow where the ability to fail once was.

Keep reminding me, and I will keep
reminding you. Remember that
you cannot tell east from west, remember
that in separate cars, you leading
and then I leading, it once
took us two hours to find the freeway.
Remember the Christmas Day in Bucks County
when I was trying to call Seattle, and
the long-distance operator began to try
to put long-distance calls through me
in the upstairs bedroom,
and when I explained I was only trying
to call Seattle, said: "You poor thing."

Even if the money comes, let us be poor
and spend it rapidly on British Leyland
motor cars that collapse when scolded
and on fish poachers for which we have

no fish. And after the banquet
at which multiples of ourselves have toasted
multiples of ourselves many times over
and turned red in the face, let us go back
to a shabby hotel room and talk
about what went wrong, and remember
how dangerous it is to be right, and how
dangerous to be powerful, even in small things.

Twentieth Century

ALFONSINA STORNI

Translated from the Spanish
by Marion Freeman

I am being consumed by life
Wasting, not doing anything,
Between the four symmetrical
Walls of my house.

Oh, workers! Bring your picks!
Let my walls and roof fall,
Let air move my blood,
Let sun burn my shoulders.

I am a twentieth-century woman.
I spend my day lounging,
Watching, from my room,
How a branch moves.

Europe is burning,
And I'm watching its flames
With the same indifference
With which I contemplate that branch.

You, passerby, don't look me
Up and down; my soul
Shouts its crime aloud, yours
Hides under its words.

What Happens

ERICH FRIED

Translated from the German
by Michael Hamburger

*I*t has happened
and it happens now as before
and will continue to happen
if nothing is done against it

The innocent don't know a thing about it
because they're too innocent
and the guilty don't know a thing about it
because they're too guilty

The poor don't notice it
because they're too poor
and the rich don't notice it
because they're too rich

The stupid shrug their shoulders
because they're too stupid
and the clever shrug their shoulders
because they're too clever

It doesn't bother the young
because they're too young
and it doesn't bother the old
because they're too old

That's why nothing is done against it
and that's why it happened
and happens now as before
and will continue to happen

 IV

TO BE OF USE

Action and Compassion

Small Frogs Killed on the Highway

JAMES WRIGHT

Still,
I would leap too
Into the light,
If I had the chance.
It is everything, the wet green stalk of the field
On the other side of the road.
They crouch there, too, faltering in terror
And take strange wing. Many
Of the dead never moved, but many
Of the dead are alive forever in the split second
Auto headlights more sudden
Than their drivers know.
The drivers burrow backward into dank pools
Where nothing begets
Nothing.

Across the road, tadpoles are dancing
On the quarter thumbnail
Of the moon. They can't see,
Not yet.

To be of use

❦ MARGE PIERCY

The people I love the best
jump into work head first
without dallying in the shallows
and swim off with sure strokes almost out of sight.
They seem to become natives of that element,
the black sleek heads of seals
bouncing like half-submerged balls.

I love people who harness themselves, an ox to a
    heavy cart,
who pull like water buffalo, with massive patience,
who strain in the mud and the muck to move things
    forward,
who do what has to be done, again and again.

I want to be with people who submerge
in the task, who go into the fields to harvest
and work in a row and pass the bags along,
who are not parlor generals and field deserters
but move in a common rhythm
when the food must come in or the fire be put out.

The work of the world is common as mud.
Botched, it smears the hands, crumbles to dust.
But the thing worth doing well done
has a shape that satisfies, clean and evident.
Greek amphoras for wine or oil,

Hopi vases that held corn, are put in museums
but you know they were made to be used.
The pitcher cries for water to carry
and a person for work that is real.

On Living (Part I)

NAZIM HIKMET

*Translated from the Turkish
by Randy Blasing and Mutlu Konuk*

I.

Living is no laughing matter:
    you must live with great seriousness
        like a squirrel, for example—
I mean without looking for something beyond
    and above living,
        I mean living must be your
          whole occupation.
Living is no laughing matter:
        you must take it seriously,
        so much so and to such a
        degree
    that, for example, your hands tied behind
    your back,
        your back to the wall,
or else in a laboratory

in your white coat and safety glasses,
you can die for people—
even for people whose faces you've never seen,
even though you know living
is the most real, the most
beautiful thing.
I mean, you must take living so seriously
that even at seventy, for example, you'll plant
olive trees—
and not for your children, either,
but because although you fear death you don't
believe it,
because living, I mean, weighs heavier.

Her Head

❧ JOAN MURRAY

*N*ear Ekuvukeni,
in Natal, South Africa,
a woman carries water on her head.
After a year of drought,
when one child in three is at risk of death,
she returns from a distant well,
carrying water on her head.

The pumpkins are gone,
the tomatoes withered,
yet the woman carries water on her head.
The cattle kraals are empty,
the goats gaunt—
no milk now for children,
but *she* is carrying water on her head.

The engineers have reversed the river:
those with power can keep their power,
but *one* woman is carrying water on her head.

In the homelands, where the dusty crowds
watch the empty roads for water trucks,
one woman trusts herself with treasure,
and carries the water on her head.

The sun does not dissuade her,
not the dried earth that blows against her,
as she carries the water on her head.
In a huge and dirty pail,
with an idle handle,
resting on a narrow can,
this *woman* is carrying water on her head.

This woman, who girds her neck
with safety pins, this one
who carries water on her head,
trusts her *own* head to bring to her people
what they need now
between life and death:
She is carrying them water on her head.

Nocturnal Visits

∾ CLARIBEL ALEGRÍA

*Translated from the
Spanish by D. J. Flakoll*

I think of our anonymous boys
of our burnt-out heroes
the amputated
the cripples
those who lost both legs
both eyes
the stammering teenagers.
At night I listen to their phantoms
shouting in my ear
shaking me out of lethargy
issuing me commands.
I think of their tattered lives
of their feverish hands
reaching out to seize ours.
It's not that they're begging
they're demanding

they've earned the right to order us
to break up our sleep
to come awake
to shake off once and for all
this lassitude.

The Dream

〰 WILLIAM MATTHEWS

A bare hill. Above it, the early evening sky, a flat,
blue-gray slate color like a planetarium ceiling
before the show's begun. Just over the hill and rising,
like a moon, the stuttering thwack of helicopter rotors

and then from behind the hill the machine itself
came straight up and stood in the air like a tossed
ball stopped at its zenith. It shone a beam of light
on me and a voice that seemed to travel through

the very beam intoned—that's the right word,
intoned—*We know where you are and we can find
you anytime. Don't write that poem. You know the one
we mean.* Then all was gone—the voice, the beam,

the helicopter and the dream. I'd lain down for a nap
that afternoon and slept through dusk. Outside the sky
was flat, blue-gray and slate. I'd no idea what poem
they meant. I lay swaddled in sweat five minutes

or an hour, I don't know. I made coffee and walked,
each muscle sprung like a trap, as far as the bridge
over the falls. I'd have said my mind was empty,
or thronged with dread, but now I understand

that in some way I also don't know how to say
I was composing with each trudge these words.
Until I steal from fear and silence what I'm not
supposed to say, these words will have to do.

Perhaps...

SHU TING

Translated from the
Chinese by Carolyn Kizer

for the loneliness of an author

Perhaps these thoughts of ours
               will never find an audience
Perhaps the mistaken road
               will end in a mistake
Perhaps the lamps we light one at a time
               will be blown out, one at a time
Perhaps the candles of our lives will gutter out
               without lighting a fire to warm us.

Perhaps when all the tears have been shed
               the earth will be more fertile
Perhaps when we sing praises to the sun
               the sun will praise us in return
Perhaps these heavy burdens
               will strengthen our philosophy

Perhaps when we weep for those in misery
                    we must be silent about miseries of our own

Perhaps
Because of our irresistible sense of mission
We have no choice

On the Threshold

Eugenio Montale

*Translated from the Italian
by Jonathan Galassi*

*B*e happy if the wind inside the orchard
carries back the tidal surge of life:
here, where a dead web
of memories sinks under,
was no garden, but a reliquary.

The whir you're hearing isn't flight,
but the stirring of the eternal womb;
watch this solitary strip of land
transform into a crucible.

There's fury over the sheer wall.
If you move forward you may come upon
the phantom who will save you:
histories are shaped here, deeds
the endgame of the future will dismantle.

Look for a flaw in the net that binds us
tight, burst through, break free!
Go, I've prayed for this for you—now my thirst
will be easy, my rancor less bitter . . .

V

THEY SAID

Leaders and Politicians

They Said

∽ REG SANER

*T*hey said "Listen class attention before sorting
your blocks put the red ones in the tray
and yellow in the bowl." So most got all but one
or two of them right and drank paper cups
of pre-sweetened juice voting later to stuff
them nicely down the trash-clown on the way home.

They said, "Now color the Holy Manger brown
the Virgin Mary blue the Christ child pink
and St. Joseph anything you like." So this one boy
colored him polka-dot but was allowed to try again
on a fresh sheet getting a green paper star on his
second St. Joseph he colored him pink a suitable choice.

They said "Democracy is at the crossroads everyone
will be given a gun and a map in cases like this
there is no need to vote." Our group scored quite

well getting each of its villages right except
one but was allowed to try again on a fresh village
we colored it black and then wore our brass
stars of unit citation almost all the way home.

As the President Spoke

〰 TED KOOSER

*A*s the President spoke, he raised a finger
to emphasize something he said. I've forgotten
just what he was saying, but as he spoke
he glanced at that finger as if it were
somebody else's, and his face went slack and gray,
and he folded his finger back into its hand
and put it down under the podium
along with whatever it meant, with whatever he'd
        seen
as it spun out and away from that bony axis.

"next to of course god america i

∿ E. E. CUMMINGS

"next to of course god america i
love you land of the pilgrims' and so forth oh
say can you see by the dawn's early my
country 'tis of centuries come and go
and are no more what of it we should worry
in every language even deafanddumb
thy sons acclaim your glorious name by gorry
by jingo by gee by gosh by gum
why talk of beauty what could be more beaut-
iful than these heroic happy dead
who rushed like lions to the roaring slaughter
they did not stop to think they died instead
then shall the voice of liberty be mute?"

He spoke.   And drank rapidly a glass of water

Waiting for the Barbarians

C. P. CAVAFY

*Translated from the Greek
by Edmund Keeley and Philip Sherrard*

What are we waiting for, assembled in the forum?

    The barbarians are due here today.

Why isn't anything going on in the senate?
Why are the senators sitting there without legislating?

    Because the barbarians are coming today.
    What's the point of senators making laws now?
    Once the barbarians are here, they'll do the legislating.

Why did our emperor get up so early,
and why is he sitting enthroned at the city's main gate,
in state, wearing the crown?

Because the barbarians are coming today
and the emperor's waiting to receive their leader.
He's even got a scroll to give him,
loaded with titles, with imposing names.

Why have our two consuls and praetors come out
        today
wearing their embroidered, their scarlet togas?
Why have they put on bracelets with so many
        amethysts,
rings sparkling with magnificent emeralds?
Why are they carrying elegant canes
beautifully worked in silver and gold?

    Because the barbarians are coming today
    and things like that dazzle the barbarians.

Why don't our distinguished orators turn up as usual
to make their speeches, say what they have to say?

    Because the barbarians are coming today
    and they're bored by rhetoric and public speaking.

Why this sudden bewilderment, this confusion?
(How serious people's faces have become.)
Why are the streets and squares emptying so rapidly,
everyone going home lost in thought?

>   Because night has fallen and the barbarians haven't
>   come.
>   And some of our men just in from the border say
>   there are no barbarians any longer.

Now what's going to happen to us without barbarians?
Those people were a kind of solution.

FROM *The Teeth Mother Naked at Last*

〰 ROBERT BLY

* * *

The ministers lie, the professors lie, the television
    reporters lie, the priests lie.
What are these lies? They mean that the country
    wants to die.
Lie after lie starts out into the prairie grass,
like mile-long caravans of Conestoga wagons
    crossing the Platte.

And a long desire for death goes with them, guiding
    it all from beneath:
"a death longing if all longing else be vain,"
stringing together the vague and foolish words.

It is a desire to eat death,
to gobble it down,
to rush on it like a cobra with mouth open.
It is a desire to take death inside,

to feel it burning inside, pushing out velvety hairs,
like a clothesbrush in the intestines—

That is the thrill that leads the President on to lie.

* * *

Now the Chief Executive enters, and the press
    conference begins.
First the President lies about the date the Appalachian
    Mountains rose.
Then he lies about the population of Chicago,
then the weight of the adult eagle, and the acreage
    of the Everglades.
Next he lies about the number of fish taken every year in
    the Arctic.

He has private information about which city *is* the
    capital of Wyoming.
He lies next about the birthplace of Attila the Hun,
Then about the composition of the amniotic fluid.

He insists that Luther was never a German,
and only the Protestants sold indulgences.
He declares that Pope Leo X *wanted* to reform the
    Church, but the liberal elements prevented him.

He declares the Peasants' War was fomented by Italians
    from the North.
And the Attorney General lies about the time the sun
    sets.

          * * *

These lies mean that something in the nation wants
    to die.

What is there now to hold us to earth? We long to go.
It is the longing for someone to come and take us by the
    hand to where they all are sleeping:
where the Egyptian pharaohs are asleep, and our own
    mothers,
and all those disappeared children, who went around
    with us on the rings at grade school.

Do not be angry at the President—
He is longing to take in his hands the locks of
    death-hair:
to meet his own children, dead, or never born. . . .

He is drifting sideways toward the dusty places.

"For Those Dead, Our Dead..."

ᘓ ERNESTO CARDENAL

Translated from the Spanish
by Jonathan Cohen

*W*hen you get the nomination, the award, the
   promotion,
think about the ones who died.
When you are at the reception, on the delegation,
   on the commission,
think about the ones who died.
When you have won the vote, and the crowd
   congratulates you,
think about the ones who died.
When you're cheered as you go up to the speaker's
   platform with the leaders,
think about the ones who died.
When you're picked up at the airport in the big city,
think about the ones who died.
When it's your turn to talk into the microphone,
   when the tv cameras focus on you,
think about the ones who died.

When you become the one who gives out the certificates,
    orders, permission,
think about the ones who died.
When the little old lady comes to you with her problem,
    her little piece of land,
think about the ones who died.
        See them without their shirts, being dragged,
    gushing blood, wearing hoods, blown to pieces,
submerged in tubs, getting electric shocks,
                        their eyes gouged out,
        their throats cut, riddled with bullets,
dumped along the side of the road,
        in holes they dug themselves,
        in mass graves,
or just lying on the ground, enriching the soil of wild
    plants:
You represent them.
The ones who died
delegated you.

The Last Election

John Haines

Suppose there are no returns,
and the candidates, one
by one, drop off in the polls,
as the voters turn away,
each to his inner persuasion.

The front runners, the dark horses,
begin to look elsewhere,
and even the President admits
he has nothing new to say;
it is best to be silent now.

No more conventions, no donors,
no more hats in the ring;
no ghost-written speeches,
no promises we always knew
were never meant to be kept.

And something like the truth,
or what we knew by that name—
that for which no corporate
sponsor was ever offered—
takes hold in the public mind.

Each subdued and thoughtful
citizen closes his door, turns
off the news. He opens a book,
speaks quietly to his children,
begins to live once more.

Last-Minute Message for a Time Capsule

    Philip Appleman

I have to tell you this, whoever you are:
that on one summer morning here, the ocean
pounded in on tumbledown breakers,
a south wind, bustling along the shore,
whipped the froth into little rainbows,
and a reckless gull swept down the beach
as if to fly were everything it needed.
I thought of your hovering saucers,
looking for clues, and I wanted to write this down,
so it wouldn't be lost forever—
that once upon a time we had
meadows here, and astonishing things,
swans and frogs and luna moths
and blue skies that could stagger your heart.
We could have had them still,
and welcomed you to earth, but
we also had the righteous ones

who worshipped the True Faith and Holy War.
When you go home to your shining galaxy,
say that what you learned
from this dead and barren place is
to beware the righteous ones.

VI

A PRAYER THAT
WILL BE ANSWERED

*Meditation
and Prayer*

The Task

JANE HIRSHFIELD

It is a simple garment, this slipped-on world.
We wake into it daily—open eyes, braid hair—
a robe unfurled
in rose-silk flowering, then laid bare.

And yes, it is a simple enough task
we've taken on,
though also vast:
from dusk to dawn,

from dawn to dusk, to praise, and not
be blinded by the praising.
To lie like a cat in hot
sun, fur fully blazing,

and dream the mouse;
and to keep too the mouse's patient, waking watch
within the deep rooms of the house,
where the leaf-flocked

sunlight never reaches, but the earth still blooms.

I Can't Speak

ALICIA OSTRIKER

God is the Being... that may properly
only be addressed, not expressed.
  —Martin Buber, *I and Thou*

It's hopeless. Our heads are full of television
But images fall apart when you enter a room.
And if not television, then words.
Poets, philosophers, intellectuals, theologians—
Can any of us truly love you?
I want to talk about kissing the small piece
Of nameless, edgeless geometry you've shown me
And how grateful I am. But should I say I'm the pond
A star fell into, or a rock?

Anyway, I can't speak about you,
Only to you, there's the whole trouble,
As if, when I tried to turn my body aside,
Some absolute force twisted it back around.

If I insist, *It's my body, my mind,*
My own mouth, I'll say what I want,
I have the right to,
You simply smile.

Eagle Poem

∾ JOY HARJO

*T*o pray you open your whole self
To sky, to earth, to sun, to moon
To one whole voice that is you
And know there is more
That you can't see, can't hear
Can't know except in moments
Steadily growing, and in languages
That aren't always sound but other
Circles of motion.
Like eagle that Sunday morning
Over Salt River. Circled in blue sky
In wind, swept our hearts clean
With sacred wings.
We see you, see ourselves and know
That we must take the utmost care
And kindness in all things.
Breathe in, knowing we are made of
All this, and breathe, knowing
We are truly blessed because we

Were born, and die soon within a
True circle of motion,
Like eagle rounding out the morning
Inside us.
We pray that it will be done
In beauty.
In beauty.

Prayer Before Birth

Louis MacNeice

I am not yet born; O hear me.
Let not the bloodsucking bat or the rat or the stoat or the
   clubfooted ghoul come near me.

I am not yet born; console me.
I fear that the human race may with tall walls wall me,
   with strong drugs dope me, with wise lies lure me,
      on black racks rack me, in blood-baths roll me.

I am not yet born; provide me
With water to dandle me, grass to grow for me, trees to talk
   to me, sky to sing to me, birds and a white light
      In the back of my mind to guide me.

I am not yet born; forgive me
For the sins that in me the world shall commit, my words
   when they speak me, my thoughts when they think me,
      my treason engendered by traitors beyond me,
         my life when they murder by means of my
            hands, my death when they live me.

I am not yet born; rehearse me
In the parts I must play and the cues I must take when
  old men lecture me, bureaucrats hector me, mountains
    frown at me, lovers laugh at me, the white
      waves call me to folly and the desert calls
        me to doom and the beggar refuses
          my gift and my children curse me.
I am not yet born; O hear me,
Let not the man who is beast or who thinks he is God come
  near me.

I am not yet born; O fill me
With strength against those who would freeze my
humanity, would dragoon me into a lethal automaton,
  would make me a cog in a machine, a thing with
    one face, a thing, and against all those
      who would dissipate my entirety, would
        blow me like thistledown hither and
          thither or hither and thither
            like water held in the
              hands would spill me
Let them not make me a stone and let them not spill me.
Otherwise kill me.

Breyten Prays for Himself

BREYTEN BREYTENBACH

*Translated from the
Afrikaans by Denis Hirson*

There is no need for Pain Lord
We could live well without it
A flower has no teeth

It is true we are only fulfilled in death
But let our flesh stay fresh as cabbage
Make us firm as pink fish
Let us tempt each other, our eyes deep butterflies

Have mercy on our mouths our bowels our brains
Let us always taste the sweetness of the evening sky
Swim in warm seas, sleep with the sun
Ride peacefully on bicycles through bright Sundays

And gradually we will decompose like old ships or
    trees
But keep Pain far from Me o Lord
That others may bear it

Be taken into custody, Shattered
Stoned
Suspended
Lashed
Used
Tortured
Crucified
Cross-examined
Placed under house arrest
Given hard labor
Banished to obscure islands till the ends of their
    days
Wasting in damp pits down to slimy green
    imploring bones
Worms in the stomachs heads full of nails
But not *Me*
But we never give Pain or complain

A Prayer That Will Be Answered

Anna Kamieńska

*Translated from the Polish by
Stanislaw Barańczak and Clare Cavanaugh*

Lord let me suffer much
and then die

Let me walk through silence
and leave nothing behind not even fear

Make the world continue
let the ocean kiss the sand just as before

Let the grass stay green
so that the frogs can hide in it

so that someone can bury his face in it
and sob out his love

Make the day rise brightly
as if there were no more pain

And let my poem stand clear as a windowpane
bumped by a bumblebee's head

O Sweet Irrational Worship

∿ THOMAS MERTON

*W*ind and a bobwhite
And the afternoon sun.

By ceasing to question the sun
I have become light,

Bird and wind.

My leaves sing.

I am earth, earth

All these lighted things
Grow from my heart.

A tall, spare pine
Stands like the initial of my first
Name when I had one.

When I had a spirit,
When I was on fire
When this valley was

Made out of fresh air
You spoke my name
In naming Your silence:
O sweet, irrational worship!

I am earth, earth

My heart's love
Bursts with hay and flowers.
I am a lake of blue air
In which my own appointed place
Field and valley
Stand reflected.

I am earth, earth

Out of my grass heart
Rises the bobwhite.

Out of my nameless weeds
His foolish worship.

Fishing in the Keep of Silence

Linda Gregg

There is a hush now while the hills rise up
and God is going to sleep. He trusts the ship
of Heaven to take over and proceed beautifully
as He lies dreaming in the lap of the world.
He knows the owls will guard the sweetness
of the soul in their massive keep of silence,
looking out with eyes open or closed over
the length of Tomales Bay that the herons
conform to, whitely broad in flight, white
and slim in standing. God, who thinks about
poetry all the time, breathes happily as He
repeats to Himself: There are fish in the net,
lots of fish this time in the net of the heart.

VII

I GAVE AWAY
THAT KID

War and Violence

American Wars

URSULA K. LE GUIN

*L*ike the topaz in the toad's head
the comfort in the terrible histories
was up front, easy to find:
Once upon a time in a kingdom far away.

Even to the dreadful now of news
we listened comforted
by far timezones, languages we didn't speak,
the wide, forgetful oceans.

Today, no comfort but the jewel courage.
The war is ours, now, here it is our republic
facing its own betraying terror.
And how we tell the story is forever after.

Fresco: Departure for an Imperialist War

❧ THOMAS McGRATH

*T*hey stand there weeping in the stained daylight.
Nothing can stop them now from reaching the end
   of their youth.

Somewhere the Mayor salutes a winning team.
Somewhere the diplomats kiss in the long corridors
   of history.

Somewhere a politician is grafting a speech
On the green tree of American money.

Somewhere prayer; somewhere orders and papers.
Somewhere the poor are gathering illegal arms.

Meanwhile they are there on that very platform.
The train sails silently toward them out of American sleep,

And at last the two are arrived at the very point of
    departure.
He goes toward death and she toward loneliness.

Weeping, their arms embrace the only country they love.

Conscientious Objector

❧ EDNA ST. VINCENT MILLAY

I shall die, but that is all that I shall do for Death.

I hear him leading his horse out of the stall; I hear
the clatter on the barn-floor.
He is in haste; he has business in Cuba, business in
the Balkans, many calls to make this morning.
But I will not hold the bridle while he cinches the
girth.
And he may mount by himself: I will not give him
a leg up.

Though he flick my shoulders with his whip, I will
not tell him which way the fox ran.
With his hoof on my breast, I will not tell him
where the black boy hides in the swamp.
I shall die, but that is all that I shall do for Death;
I am not on his pay-roll.

I will not tell him the whereabouts of my friends
    nor of my enemies either.
Though he promise me much, I will not map him
    the route to any man's door.

Am I a spy in the land of the living, that I should
    deliver men to Death?
Brother, the password and the plans of our city are
    safe with me; never through me
Shall you be overcome.

While the Record Plays

∾ GYULA ILLYÉS

Translated from the Hungarian
by William Jay Smith

*T*hey heated hatchet blades over gas fires in
    roadside workshops and hammered them
    into cleavers.

They brought wooden blocks on trucks and
    carried them across these new provinces
    grimly, quickly, and steadily: almost according
    to ritual.

Because at any time—at noon or midnight—
    they would arrive at one of these impure
    settlements,

where women did not cook nor make beds
    as theirs did, where men did not greet one
    another as they did, where children and the

whole damned company did not pronounce
words as they did, and where the girls kept
apart from them.

They would select from these insolent and
intolerable people twelve men, preferably
young ones, to take to the marketplace,

and there—because of *blah-blah-blah* and
moreover *quack-quack-quack* and likewise
quack-blah-quack—would beat and behead
them,

of historical necessity—because of *twaddle-
twiddle* and *twiddle-diddle,* and expertly,
for their occupations would be different
one from the other,

agronomist and butcher, bookbinder and engineer,
waiter and doctor, several seminarists, cadets
from military academies, a considerable number
of students,

those familiar with Carnot, Beethoven and even
Einstein, displaying their finest talents,

because, after all, nevertheless, *blah-blah-blah* and
   twiddle-dee-dee,
while through loudspeakers records played—
   music and an occasional gruff order, and they,
   the zealous ones, wiped their foreheads and
   turned aside every now and then to urinate
   since excitement affects the kidneys;

then having washed the blocks and hauled down
   the large tricolor which on such occasions
   always waved above their heads,

they too would march on into the broad future,

past the heads, carefully placed in a circle,

then out of the settlement where now also

and forever and ever,

reason, comfort, and hope would be no—

wrr-wrr-wrr—that is to say—*we-wp, wa-rp,* the
   sound (by now the only one

without music or words) that the needle makes as
   the record grinds on.

Forced March

ᐁ **MIKLÓS RADNÓTI**

*Translated from the
Hungarian by Emery George*

*T*he man who, having collapsed,   rises, takes steps,
    is insane;
he'll move an ankle, a knee,   an arrant mass of pain,
and take to the road again   as if wings were to lift
    him high;
in vain the ditch will call him: he simply dare not
    stay;
and should you ask, why not?   perhaps he'll turn
    and answer:
his wife is waiting back home,   and a death, one
    beautiful, wiser.
But see, the wretch is a fool,   for over the homes,
    that world,
long since nothing but singed   winds have been
    known to whirl;
his housewall lies supine;   your plum tree, broken
    clear,

and all the nights back home   horripilate with
    fear.
Oh, if I could believe   that I haven't merely
    borne
what is worthwhile, in my heart;   that there *is*,
    to return, a home;
tell me it's all still there: the cool verandah,
    bees
of peaceful silence buzzing,   while the plum jam
    cooled;
where over sleepy gardens   summer-end peace
    sunbathed,
and among bow and foliage   fruits were swaying
    naked;
and, blonde, my Fanni waited   before the redwood
    fence,
with morning slowly tracing   its shadowed
    reticence. . . .
But all that *could* still be—   tonight the moon
    is so round!
Don't go past me, my friend—   shout! and I'll
    come around!

Bor, 15 September 1944

I Gave Away That Kid

Grace Paley

I gave away that kid like he was an old button
    Here old button get off of me
    I don't need you anymore
    go on   get out of here
    go into the army
    sew yourself onto the colonel's shirt
    or the captain's fly   jackass
    don't you have any sense
    don't you read the papers
    why are you leaving now?

That kid walked out of here like he was the cat's pajamas
    what are you wearing pj's for   you damn fool?
    why are you crying   you couldn't
    get another job anywhere anyways
    go march to the army's drummer
    be a man like all your dead uncles
    then think of something else to do

Lost him, sorry about that   the President said
    he was a good boy
    never see one like him again
    Why don't you repeat that   your honor
    why don't you sizzle up the meaning
    of that sentence for your breakfast
    why don't you stick him in a prayer
    and count to ten before my wife gets you

That boy is a puddle in Beirut   the paper says
    scraped up for singing in church
    too bad   too bad is a terrible tune
    it's no song at all   how come you sing it?

I gave away that kid like he was an old button
    Here old button get offa me
    I don't need you anymore
    go on get out of here
    go into the army
    sew yourself onto the colonel's shirt
    or the captain's fly   jackass
    don't you have any sense
    don't you read the papers
    why are you leaving now?

"They"

Siegfried Sassoon

The Bishop tells us: 'When the boys come back
They will not be the same; for they'll have fought
In a just cause: they lead the last attack
on Anti-Christ; their comrades' blood has bought
New right to breed an honourable race,
They have challenged Death and dared him face to
     face.'

'We're none of us the same!' the boys reply.
'For George lost both his legs; and Bill's stone blind;
Poor Jim's shot through the lungs and like to die;
And Bert's gone syphilitic: you'll not find
A chap who's served that hasn't found *some* change.'
And the Bishop said: 'The ways of God are strange!'

Every Day

INGEBORG BACHMAN

*Translated from the
German by Peter Filkins*

War is no longer declared,
but rather continued. The outrageous
has become the everyday. The hero
is absent from the battle. The weak
are moved into the firing zone.
The uniform of the day is patience,
the order of merit is the wretched star
of hope over the heart.

It is awarded
when nothing more happens,
when the bombardment is silenced,
when the enemy has become invisible
and the shadow of eternal weapons
covers the sky.

It is awarded
for deserting the flag,
for bravery before a friend,
for the betrayal of shameful secrets
and the disregard
of every command.

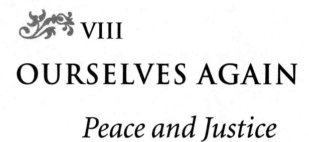 VIII

OURSELVES AGAIN

Peace and Justice

—*When They Sleep*

ROLF JACOBSEN

*Translated from the
Norwegian by Robert Hedin*

All people are children when they sleep.
There's no war in them then.
They open their hands and breathe
in that quiet rhythm heaven has given them.

They pucker their lips like small children
and open their hands halfway,
soldiers and statesmen, servants and masters.
The stars stand guard
and a haze veils the sky,
a few hours when no one will do anybody harm.

If only we could speak to one another then
when our hearts are half-open flowers.
Words like golden bees
would drift in.
—God, teach me the language of sleep.

Sabbath Poem I (1979)

WENDELL BERRY

I go among trees and sit still.
All my stirring becomes quiet
around me like circles on water.
My tasks lie in their places
where I left them, asleep like cattle.

Then what is afraid of me comes
and lives a while in my sight.
What it fears in me leaves me,
and the fear of me leaves it.
It sings, and I hear its song.

Then what I am afraid of comes.
I live for a while in its sight.
What I fear in it leaves it,
and the fear of it leaves me.
It sings, and I hear its song.

After days of labor,
mute in my consternations,
I hear my song at last,
and I sing it. As we sing,
the day turns, the trees move.

Hidden Justice

❧ GERALD STERN

This is my forest now, this Christmas cactus,
stretching out leaf after leaf,
pink blossom after pink blossom.
This is where I'll go to breathe
and live in darkness
and sit like a frog, and sit like a salamander,
and this is where I'll find a tiny light
and have my vision
and start my school—
in this dry and airy place
beside these trunks
in this fragrant mixture.

I will put my small stage here
under a thick leaf
and I will eat and sleep and preach right here
and put my two dogs there
to keep my two guards busy
with prayer and feeding.

I will live completely for the flowering,
my neck like a swan's,
my fingers clawing the air
looking for justice;
year after year the same,
my fingers clawing the air for hidden justice.

Ourselves Again
FROM *There Will Be a Better Time*

MONGANE SEROTE

* * *

*t*ime has run out for those who ride on others
if the we is the most of us
and the most of us is the will
the will to say no!
when the most of us will create a better time
there will be a better time
when time has run out for liars
for those who take and take and take from others,
    take forever!
and keep taking
for themselves alone
take and take and take
time has run out
when we say no!

no more—
—no more is not a word but an act, remember that—
my little friend
no more starts with learning to learn
learn to carry the past
like we do with dirty clothes
carry them to the washing place and wash them
we carry the past to the present
and wash it by learning what it means
when what it means becomes our action
because we have learnt it
like you learn two plus two is four
so you can count four if you have four sweets
we use the past we learnt like that
we say grandma and grandpa and pa and ma come
    from here
we are born here, so we are here
here is our land.

What I Leave to My Son

Du Tu Le

Translated from the
Vietnamese by Nguyen Ngoc Bich

No point in leaving you a long list
of those who have died:
Even if I limit it to my friends and your uncles
it won't do. Who could remember them all?
My son, isn't it true?
The obituaries leave me indifferent
as the weather: Sometimes they seem to matter
even less: How can that be, my son?

I'll leave you, yes,
a treasure I'm always seeking, never finding.
Can you guess? Something wondrous,
something my father wanted for me
although (poor man!) it's been nothing
but a mirage in the desert
of my life.
My soul will join his now, praying

that your generation may find it—
simply peace—
simply a life better than ours
where you and your friends won't be forced
to drag grief-laden feet down the road
to mutual murder.

Someone

༄ NELLY SACHS

*Translated from the German
by Ruth and Matthew Mead*

Someone
will take the ball
from the hands that play
the game of terror.

Stars
have their own law of fire
and their fertility
is the light
and reapers and harvesters
are not native here.

Far off
stand their granaries
straw too
has a momentary power of illumination
painting loneliness.

Someone will come
and sew the green of the spring bud
on their prayer shawl
and set the child's silken curl
as a sign
on the brow of the century.

Here Amen
must be said
this crowning of words
which moves into hiding
and
peace
you great eyelid
closing on all unrest
your heavenly wreath of lashes

You most gentle of all births.

The Season of Phantasmal Peace

DEREK WALCOTT

Then all the nations of birds lifted together
the huge net of the shadows of this earth
in multitudinous dialects, twittering tongues,
stitching and crossing it. They lifted up
the shadows of long pines down trackless slopes,
the shadows of glass-faced towers down evening
    streets,
the shadow of a frail plant on a city sill—
the net rising soundless as night, the birds' cries
    soundless, until
there was no longer dusk, or season, decline, or
    weather,
only this passage of phantasmal light
that not the narrowest shadow dared to sever.

And men could not see, looking up, what the wild
    geese drew,
what the ospreys trailed behind them in silvery ropes
that flashed in the icy sunlight; they could not hear

battalions of starlings waging peaceful cries,
bearing the net higher, covering this world
like the vines of an orchard, or a mother drawing
the trembling gauze over the trembling eyes
of a child fluttering to sleep;

                            it was the light
that you will see at evening on the side of a hill
in yellow October, and no one hearing knew
what change had brought into the raven's cawing,
the killdeer's screech, the ember-circling chough
such an immense, soundless, and high concern
for the fields and cities where the birds belong,
except it was their seasonal passing, Love,
made seasonless, or, from the high privilege of their
    birth,
something brighter than pity for the wingless ones
below them who shared dark holes in windows and in
    houses
and higher they lifted the net with soundless voices
above all change, betrayals of falling suns,
and this season lasted one moment, like the pause
between dusk and darkness, between fury and peace,
but, for such as our earth is now, it lasted long.

The Place Where We Are Right

YEHUDA AMICHAI

Translated from the
Hebrew by Stephen Mitchell

From the place where we are right
flowers will never grow
in the spring.

The place where we are right
is hard and trampled
like a yard.

But doubts and loves
dig up the world
like a mole, a plow.
And a whisper will be heard in the place
where the ruined
house once stood.

CREDITS

Claribel Alegría: "Nocturnal Visits," from *Fugues*. Copyright © 1993 by Claribel Alegría. Reprinted by permission of Curbstone Press. Distributed by Consortium. Yehuda Amichai: "The Place Where We Are Right," translated by Stephen Mitchell, from *The Selected Poetry of Yehuda Amichai*. Copyright © 1986, 1996 by Chana Bloch and Stephen Mitchell. Reprinted by permission of The University of California Press. Maggie Anderson: "Heart Labor," from *Windfall*, by Maggie Anderson, © 2000. Reprinted by permission of the University of Pittsburgh Press. Philip Appleman: "Last-Minute Message for a Time Capsule," from *New and Selected Poems, 1956–1996*. Published by University of Arkansas Press. Copyright © 1996 by Philip Appleman. Reprinted by permission of the author. Ingeborg Bachman: "Every Day," translated by Peter Filkins, from *Darkness Spoken: The Collected Poems of Ingeborg Bachman*. Copyright © 1994, 2005 by Peter Filkins. Reprinted by permission of Zephyr Press. Wendell Berry: "Sabbath Poem I (1979)," from *A Timbered Choir*. Copyright © 1998 by Wendell Berry. Reprinted by permission of Counterpoint Press, a member of Perseus Books, L.L.C. Robert Bly: from "The Teeth Mother Naked at Last," from *Sleepers Joining Hands*. Published by HarperCollins, New York. Copyright © 1973 by Robert Bly. Reprinted by permission of the author. Breyten Breytenbach: "Breyten Prays for Himself," from *And Death White as Words*. Published by J. M. Meulenhoff. Copyright © Breyten Breytenbach. Reprinted by permission of the author. Ernesto Cardenal: " 'For Those Dead, Our Dead . . . ,' " translated by Jonathan Cohen, from *From Nicaragua, with Love: Poems, 1979–1986*. Published by City Lights. Originally appeared in *The American Voice* (1986). Copyright © 1987 by Jonathan Cohen. Reprinted by permission of Jonathan Cohen. C. P. Cavafy: "Waiting for the Barbarians," translated by Edmund Keeley, from *C. P. Cavafy*. © 1975 by Edmund Keeley and Philip Sherrard. Reprinted by permission of Princeton University Press. David Cope: "Crash," from *Quiet Lives*. Published by Humana Press, Totowa, New Jersey. Copyright © 1983 by David Cope. Reprinted by permission of the author. William Dickey: "Those Destroyed by Success" originally appeared in *Poetry*. Copyright © 1982 by William Dickey. Reprinted by permission of the Estate of William Dickey. Rita Dove: *from* "Twelve Chairs," from *American Smooth*. Copyright © 2004 by Rita Dove. Reprinted by permission of W. W. Norton & Company, Inc. Stephen Dunn: "Scruples," from *Riffs and Reciprocities: Prose Pairs*. Copyright © 1998 by Stephen Dunn. Reprinted by permission of W. W. Norton & Company, Inc. Erich Fried: "The Measures Taken," translated by Michael Hamburger, from *99 Poems in Translation*. Copyright © 1977 by Michael Hamburger. Reprinted by permission of Michael Hamburger. Erich Fried: "What Happens," translated by Michael Hamburger from

ACKNOWLEDGMENTS

I want to acknowledge a debt of thanks to everyone at Beacon Press, and in particular to my editor, Amy Caldwell, for the vision and prodigious labor it took to bring *Poems to Live By in Uncertain Times* to readers in 2001, when it was so sorely needed. Brian Halley must be singled out as well. Yet it was the sleepless efforts of everyone (Editorial, Production, and Marketing) that made the book such an immediate and continuing success—as well as something of a legend in the publishing industry.

I'm indeed fortunate to have that same kind of vision and commitment behind *Poems to Live By in Troubling Times*. My gratitude goes to everyone I've mentioned and also to Tracy Ahlquist, who has joined the team. The troubling times we now face as a people haven't come upon us so suddenly as September 11 did, but the way out of them will similarly be a long, challenging, and vigilant one. This book will be of help, and I'm grateful to all who have helped it come into being.

I'm especially grateful to the poets whose poems I've gathered, to the translators who have made them available, and to the publishers who have given permission for their use.